*Mysteries of
the Sacraments*

By
Annie Besant

Copyright © 2023 Lamp of Trismegistus. All rights reserved. No part of this publication may be reproduced or transmitted in any form or by any means, electronic or mechanical, including photocopying, recording, or by any information storage and retrieval system, without permission in writing from Lamp of Trismegistus. Reviewers may quote brief passages.

ISBN: 978-1-63118-636-3

Esoteric Classics

Other Books in this Series and Related Titles

Hypnotism and Mesmerism by Annie Besant (978–1–63118–587–8)

The Hidden Language of Symbolism by Annie Besant (978–1–63118–585–4)

Memory and Consciousness by Besant & Blavatsky (978–1–63118–582–3)

Occultism, Semi-Occultism & Pseudo Occultism by A Besant (978–1–63118–577–9)

Spiritual Life for Man by Annie Besant (978–1–63118–573–1)

The Mysteries by Annie Besant (978–1–63118–572–4)

Communication Between Different Worlds by Annie Besant (978–1–63118–569–4)

The Brotherhood of Religions by Annie Besant (978–1–63118–563–2)

Clairvoyance and Psychic Abilities by A Besant &c (978-1-63118-403-1)

Spiritual Progress and Practical Occultism by H P Blavatsky (978–1–63118–583–0)

Alchemy in the Nineteenth Century by Helena P. Blavatsky (978-1-63118-446-8)

Rosicrucians and Speculative Masonry in the Seventeenth Century (978-1-63118-489-5)

Qabbalistic Teachings and the Tree of Life by M P Hall (978-1-63118-482-6)

Early Masonic Symbolism by Manly P Hall (978–1–63118–606–6)

Fortune-Telling with Dice by Astra Cielo (978-1-63118-466-6)

History, Analysis and Secret Tradition of the Tarot by Hall &c (978-1-63118-445-1)

Crystal Vision Through Crystal Gazing by Frater Achad (978-1-63118-455-0)

Arcane Formulas or Mental Alchemy by W W Atkinson (978-1-63118-459-8)

The Machinery of the Mind by Dion Fortune (978-1-63118-451-2)

The A E Waite Reader: A Selection of Occult Essays (978-1-63118-515-1)

The Leadbeater Reader: A Selection of Occult Essays (978-1-63118-483-3)

Audio versions are also available on Audible, Amazon and Apple

Other Books in this Series and Related Titles

Spiritualism and Theosophy by Henry S. Olcott (978-1-63118-629-5)

Duties of a Theosophist by Annie Besant (978-1-63118-628-8)

The Book of the Nephilim by Enoch (978-1-63118-627-1)

Building Occult Character by Besant & Leadbeater (978-1-63118-626-4)

Ancient Egyptian Mysteries and Hieroglyphics, Modern Freemasonry & Initiation of the Pyramid (978-1-63118-625-7) HC

The Lost Book of Noah by Noah (978-1-63118-624-0)

The Acts of Saint Andrew by Andrew (978-1-63118-623-3)

The Acts of the Apostle John by John (978–1–63118–622–6)

Karmic Visions by Helena P. Blavatsky (978–1–63118–621–9)

The Ascension of Isaiah by Isaiah (978-1-63118-620-2)

The Mysteries of Mithra by G R S Mead (978-1-63118-619-6)

Second Book of Enoch by Enoch (978-1-63118-617-2)

Lost Keys of Freemasonry by Manly P Hall (978-1-63118-616-5)

Book of the Watchers by Enoch (978-1-63118-615-8)

Sepher Yetzirah and the Qabalah by Manly P Hall (978-1-63118-614-1)

Philosophy of Self-Knowledge by Franz Hartmann (978-1-63118-613-4)

Occult Symbolism of the Sun and Moon, the Goddess Isis and thee Solar Deities by Manly P Hall (978–1–63118–611–0)

Practical Theosophy by Annie Besant (978–1–63118–610–3)

The Human Body in Symbolism by Manly P Hall (978–1–63118–609–7)

Theosophical Basics by William Q Judge (978–1–63118–608–0)

Audio versions are also available on Audible, Amazon and Apple

Table of Contents

Introduction…7

Annie Besant:
A Luminary of Theosophy and Esotericism…9

Mysteries of the Sacraments…13

INTRODUCTION

The word "esoteric" can be difficult to define. Esotericism in general can be seen less as a system of beliefs and more as a category, which encompasses numerous, different systems of beliefs. It's a bit of juxtaposition, since the word "esoteric" indicates something that few people know about, while the term itself broadly covers numerous philosophies, practices, areas of study and belief systems.

In a greater sense, Esotericism acts as a storehouse for secret knowledge, which is often considered ancient *(by tradition, if not by fact)*, passed down from generation to generation, in private. At various times in history, simply possessing the knowledge of some of these subjects, was considered illegal and a jailable offence, if discovered. This usually included such general topics as Alchemy, Pharmacology, Qabalah, Hermeticism, Occultism, Ceremonial Magic, Astrology, Divination, Rosicrucianism and so on. Collectively, these areas of study were often referred to as the esoteric sciences.

Sometimes, the outer garment of a subject isn't esoteric, while what is hidden beneath it, is. As an example, Freemasonry isn't necessarily esoteric by nature *(at least not anymore)*, but certain signs, passwords and handshakes given to the candidate during their initiation, are in fact, esoteric, in the sense that they are hidden from the general public.

Today, in the twenty-first century, such topics are readily available at bookstores across the country, and numerous main-steam publishers offer beginners guides and coffee-table volumes on many of these subjects, intended for mass appeal. Books like *"The Secret"* have turned previously arcane topics into household knowledge. All that being the case, however, it isn't to say that there still aren't buried secrets to uncover, ancient wisdom being ignored and forgotten mysteries to be explored. In fact, it is often that we are only able to further our own studies by standing on the shoulders of these disappearing giants.

Lamp of Trismegistus is doing its part to help preserve humanity's esoteric history by making some of these classics available to those students who are seeking to unearth the knowledge of these ancient colossi.

So, be sure to check other titles from our *Esoteric Classics* series, as well as our *Occult Fiction, Theosophical Classics, Foundations of Freemasonry Series, Studies in Alchemy, Supernatural Fiction, Paranormal Research Series, Studies in Buddhism* and our *Christian Apocrypha Series*. You can also download the audio versions of most of these titles from Amazon, Apple or Audible, for learning on the go.

ANNIE BESANT: A LUMINARY OF THEOSOPHY AND ESOTERICISM

Annie Besant, a significant figure in the spiritual milieu of the 19th and 20th centuries, represents a unique blend of activism, education, and spiritual exploration. She is perhaps best known for her pivotal role in the Theosophical Society, which was committed to studying comparative religion, philosophy, and science, and promoting the universal brotherhood of humanity. However, Besant's interest in and contributions to Theosophy and the occult, as well as her other esoteric connections, provide a deeper understanding of her life and work.

Born on October 1, 1847, in London, Besant's early life was deeply influenced by a rigorous religious education, which spurred a lifelong quest for spiritual and philosophical truth. However, it wasn't until her introduction to the works of Helena Petrovna Blavatsky, the co-founder of the Theosophical Society with Henry S. Olcott, that Besant found a framework that resonated deeply with her own esoteric leanings.

Joining the Theosophical Society in 1889 marked a turning point in Besant's life. Her keen intellect and voracious curiosity made her a natural fit for the society, and she soon emerged as a leading figure within the organization; in fact, Besant's encounters with Blavatsky and Olcott led to profound transformations in her personal and intellectual life and played a crucial role in shaping her future as a theosophist.

Besant's initial introduction to theosophy was through her encounters with Blavatsky's writings. The book "The Secret Doctrine," Blavatsky's magnum opus, was particularly influential. The text's exploration of the synthesis of science, religion, and philosophy intrigued Besant, sparking a desire to explore these concepts further. Besant was deeply moved by the central tenets of theosophy – universal brotherhood, the study of comparative religion, philosophy, and science, and the investigation of the unexplained laws of nature and the powers latent in humanity.

Intrigued by these ideas, Besant met with Blavatsky in 1889, marking the beginning of a relationship that would significantly shape her spiritual path. Blavatsky recognized Besant's potential and quickly became her mentor, guiding her into the theosophical fold. Besant, impressed by Blavatsky's intellect and spiritual insight, described her as a "great teacher" and a "friend."

Under Blavatsky's guidance, Besant rapidly advanced within the Theosophical Society, with her intellect and passion making her a natural fit for leadership roles. When Blavatsky died in 1891, Besant was among the members who were instrumental in carrying forward her legacy.

Besant's relationship with Henry Steel Olcott, the co-founder and first President of the Theosophical Society, was decidedly different but also played a significant role in her involvement with theosophy. Although Olcott was primarily based in Asia, his correspondence and occasional meetings with Besant helped deepen her understanding of theosophy and its objectives. Olcott's emphasis on practical spirituality and service, as well as his efforts to reconcile Western and Eastern spiritual traditions, deeply resonated with Besant. His influence would be seen in her later work in India, where she embraced and promoted Hindu philosophy and culture, just as Olcott had done with Buddhism in Sri Lanka.

After Olcott's death in 1907, Besant became President of the Theosophical Society, a position she held until her death in 1933. In this role, she was able to build upon the foundations laid by Blavatsky and Olcott, expanding the reach of theosophy and promoting its principles worldwide.

The relationships with Blavatsky and Olcott had a profound influence on Besant's life and work. They marked the beginning of her journey into theosophy and the esoteric, offering guidance, inspiration, and a platform for her to explore and share her spiritual insights. This trilateral bond between Besant, Blavatsky, and Olcott became a cornerstone of theosophical history, shaping not just Besant's personal journey, but also the broader trajectory of the Theosophical Society.

Besant's overall involvement in Theosophy was marked by a deep commitment to the exploration of the esoteric and the occult. She authored numerous works on these subjects, including "The Ancient Wisdom" and "Thought Power: Its Control and Culture", contributing significantly to the society's body of knowledge. These works delved into various aspects of metaphysics, spirituality, and the occult, offering comprehensive insights into the esoteric wisdom that lay at the heart of theosophy.

Throughout her tenure as leader of the Theosophical Society, Besant demonstrated a profound interest in eastern religions, particularly Hinduism and Buddhism. She believed that these ancient wisdom traditions held key insights into the nature of reality and the human spirit. Besant's efforts helped to bridge the gap between Eastern and Western spiritual thought, fostering a greater understanding and appreciation of these traditions among Western audiences.

Beyond her work in Theosophy, Besant's interests extended to various other esoteric fields. She studied and wrote about astrology, alchemy, and mysticism, drawing connections between these disciplines and theosophical thought. She also explored the realms of psychic phenomena and spiritualism, contributing to a growing body of literature on these subjects at the time.

Besant's influence extended well beyond the confines of the Theosophical Society. In India, she was deeply involved in the nation's struggle for independence, and she also contributed to the field of education by establishing the Central Hindu College in Benares, which later became a part of the Banaras Hindu University.

Annie Besant's life and work represent a remarkable fusion of spiritual exploration, esoteric scholarship, and activism. Her significant contributions to Theosophy, her insights into the occult, and her commitment to bridging the gap between Eastern and Western spiritual traditions mark her as a leading figure in the history of esoteric thought. Even today, her writings continue to inspire and guide those who venture into the realm of the spiritual and the esoteric.

MYSTERIES OF THE SACRAMENTS

In all religions there exist certain ceremonials, or rites, which are regarded as of vital importance by the believers in the religion, and which are held to confer certain benefits on those taking part in them. The word Sacrament, or some equivalent term, has been applied to these ceremonials, and they all have the same character. Little exact exposition has been given as to their nature and meaning, but this is another of the subjects explained of old in the Lesser Mysteries.

The peculiar characteristic of a Sacrament resides in two of its properties. First, there is the exoteric ceremony, which is a pictorial allegory, a representation of something by actions and materials—not a verbal allegory, a teaching given in words, conveying a truth; but an acted representation, certain definite material things used in a particular way. The object in choosing these materials, and aimed at in the ceremonies by which their manipulation is accompanied, is to represent, as in a picture, some truth which it is desired to impress upon the minds of the people present. That is the first and obvious property of a Sacrament, differentiating it from other forms of worship and meditation. It appeals to those who without this imagery would fail to catch a subtle truth, and shows to them in a vivid and graphic form the truth which otherwise would escape them. Every Sacrament, when it is studied, should be taken first from this standpoint, that it is a pictorial allegory; the essential things to be studied will therefore be: the material objects which enter into the allegory, the method in which they are employed, and the meaning which the whole is intended to convey.

The second characteristic property of a Sacrament belongs to the facts of the invisible worlds, and is studied by occult science. The person who officiates in the Sacrament should possess this knowledge, as much, though not all, of the operative power of the Sacrament depends on the knowledge of the officiator. A Sacrament links the material world with the subtle and invisible regions to which that world is related; it is a link between the visible and the invisible. And it is not only a link between this world and other worlds, but it is also a method by which the energies of the invisible world are transmuted into action in the physical; an actual method of changing energies of one kind into energies of another, as literally as in the galvanic cell chemical energies are changed into electrical. The essence of all energies is one and the same, whether in the visible or invisible worlds; but the energies differ according to the grades of matter through which they manifest. A Sacrament serves as a kind of crucible in which spiritual alchemy takes place. An energy placed in this crucible and subjected to certain manipulations comes forth different in expression. Thus an energy of a subtle kind, belonging to one of the higher regions of the universe, may be brought into direct relation with people living in the physical world, and may be made to affect them in the physical world as well as in its own realm; the Sacrament forms the last bridge from the invisible to the visible, and enables the energies to be directly applied to those who fulfil the necessary conditions and who take part in the Sacrament.

The Sacraments of the Christian Church lost much of their dignity and of the recognition of their occult power among those who separated from the Roman Catholic Church at the time of the "Reformation." The previous separation between the East and the West, leaving the Greek Orthodox Church on the one side and the Roman Church on the other, in no way affected belief in the Sacraments. They remained in both great communities as the recognised links between the seen and the unseen, and sanctified the life of the believer from cradle to grave. The Seven Sacraments of Christianity cover the whole of life, from the welcome of Baptism to the farewell of Extreme Unction. They were established by Occultists, by men who knew the invisible worlds; and the materials used, the words spoken, the signs made, were all deliberately chosen and arranged with a view to bringing about certain results.

At the time of the Reformation, the seceding Churches, which threw off the yoke of Rome, were not led by Occultists, but by ordinary men of the world, some good and some bad, but all profoundly ignorant of the facts of the invisible worlds, and conscious only of the outer shell of Christianity, its literal dogmas and exoteric worship. The consequence of this was that the Sacraments lost their supreme place in Christian worship, and in most Protestant communities were reduced to two, Baptism and the Eucharist. The sacramental nature of the others was not explicitly denied in the most important of the seceding Churches, but the two were set apart from the five, as of universal obligation, of which every member of the Church must partake in order to be recognised as a full member.

The general definition of a Sacrament is given quite accurately, save for the superfluous words, "ordained by Christ Himself," in the Catechism of the Church of England, and even these words might be retained if the mystic meaning be given to the word "Christ." A Sacrament is there said to be: "An outward and visible sign of an inward and spiritual grace given unto us, ordained by Christ Himself, as a means whereby we receive the same and a pledge to assure us thereof."

In this definition we find laid down the two distinguishing characteristics of a Sacrament as given above. The "outward and visible sign" is the pictorial allegory, and the phrase, the "means whereby we receive the" "inward and spiritual grace" covers the second property. This last phrase should be carefully noted by those members of Protestant Churches who regard Sacraments as mere external forms and outer ceremonies. For it distinctly alleges that the Sacrament is really a means whereby the grace is conveyed, and thus implies that without it the grace does not pass in the same fashion from the spiritual to the physical world. It is the distinct recognition of a Sacrament in its second aspect, as a means whereby spiritual powers are brought into activity on earth.

In order to understand a Sacrament, it is necessary that we should definitely recognise the existence of an occult, or hidden, side of Nature; this is spoken of as the life-side of Nature, the consciousness-side, more accurately the mind *in* Nature. Underlying all sacramental action there is the belief that the invisible world exercises a potent influence over the visible, and to understand a Sacrament we must understand something of the invisible Intelligences who administer Nature. We have seen in studying the doctrine of the Trinity that Spirit is manifested as the triple Self, and that as the Field for His manifestation there is Matter, the form-side of Nature, often regarded, and rightly, as Nature herself. We have to study both these aspects, the side of life and that of form, in order to understand a Sacrament.

Stretching between the Trinity and humanity are many grades and hierarchies of invisible beings; the highest of these are the seven Spirits of God, the seven Fires, or Flames, that are before the throne of God. Each of these stands at the head of a vast host of Intelligences, all of whom share His nature and act under His direction; these are themselves graded, and are the Thrones, Powers, Princes, Dominations, Archangels, Angels, of whom mention is found in the writings of the Christian Fathers, who were versed in the Mysteries. Thus there are seven great hosts of these Beings, and they represent in their intelligence the divine Mind in Nature. They are found in all regions, and they ensoul the energies of Nature. From the standpoint of occultism there is no dead force and no dead matter. Force and matter alike are living and active, and an energy or a group of energies is the veil of an Intelligence, of a Consciousness, who has that energy as his outer expression, and the matter in which that energy moves yields a form which he guides or ensouls. Unless a man can thus look at Nature all esoteric teaching must remain for him a sealed book.

Without these angelic Lives, these countless invisible Intelligences, these Consciousnesses which ensoul the force and matter which is Nature, Nature herself would not only remain unintelligible, but she would be out of relation alike to the divine Life that moves within and around her, and to the human lives that are developing in her midst. These innumerable Angels link the worlds together; they are themselves evolving while helping the evolution of beings lower than themselves, and a new light is shed on evolution when we see that men form grades in these hierarchies of intelligent beings. These angels are the "sons of God" of an earlier birth than ours, who "shouted for joy" when the foundations of the earth were laid amid the choiring of the Morning Stars.

Others beings are below us in evolution—animals, plants, minerals, and elemental lives—as the Angels are above us; and as we thus study, a conception dawns upon us of a vast Wheel of Life, of numberless existences, inter-related and necessary each to each, man as a living Intelligence, as a self-conscious being, having his own place in this Wheel. The Wheel is ever turning by the divine Will, and the living Intelligences who form it learn to co-operate with that Will, and if in the action of those Intelligences there is any break or gap due to neglect or opposition, then the Wheel drags, turning slowly, and the chariot of the evolution of the worlds goes but heavily upon its way.

These numberless Lives, above and below man, come into touch with human consciousness in very definite ways, and among these ways are sounds and colours. Each sound has a form in the invisible world, and combinations of sounds create complicated shapes. In the subtle matter of those worlds all sounds are accompanied by colours, so that they give rise to many-hued shapes, in many cases exceedingly beautiful. The vibrations set up in the visible world when a note is sounded set up vibrations in the worlds invisible, each one with its own specific character, and capable of producing certain effects. In communicating with the sub-human Intelligences connected with the lower invisible world and with the physical, and in controlling and directing these, sounds must be used fitted to bring about the desired results, as language made up of definite sounds is used here. And in communicating with the higher Intelligences certain sounds are useful, to create a harmonious atmosphere, suitable for their activities, and to make our own subtle bodies receptive of their influences.

This effect on the subtle bodies is a most important part of the occult use of sounds. These bodies, like the physical, are in constant vibratory motion, the vibrations changing with every thought or desire. These changing irregular vibrations offer an obstacle to any fresh vibration coming from outside, and, in order to render the bodies susceptible to the higher influences, sounds are used which reduce the irregular vibrations to a steady rhythm, like in its nature to the rhythm of the Intelligence sought to be reached. The object of all often-repeated sentences is to effect this, as a musician sounds the same note over and over again, until all the instruments are in tune. The subtle bodies must be tuned to the note of the Being sought, if his influence is to find free way through the nature of the worshipper, and this was ever done of old by the use of sounds. Hence, music has ever formed an integral part of worship, and certain definite cadences have been preserved with care, handed on from age to age.

In every religion there exist sounds of a peculiar character, called "Words of Power," consisting of sentences in a particular language chanted in a particular way; each religion possesses a stock of such sentences, special successions of sounds, now very generally called "mantras," that being the name given to them in the East, where the science of mantras has been much studied and elaborated. It is not necessary that a mantra—a succession of sounds arranged in a particular manner to bring about a definite result—should be in any one particular language. Any language can be used for the purpose, though some are more suitable than others, provided that the person who makes the mantra possesses the requisite occult knowledge. There are hundreds of mantras in the Samskrit tongue, made by Occultists of the past, who were familiar with the laws of the invisible worlds. These have been handed down from generation to generation, definite words in a definite order chanted in a definite way. The effect of the chanting is to create vibrations, hence forms, in the physical and super-physical worlds, and according to the knowledge and purity of the singer will be the worlds his song is able to affect If his knowledge be wide and deep, if his will be strong and his heart pure, there is scarcely any limit to the powers he may exercise in using some of these ancient mantras.

As said, it is not necessary that any one particular language should be used. They may be in Samskrit, or in any one of the languages of the world, in which men of knowledge have put them together.

This is the reason why, in the Roman Catholic Church, the Latin language is always used in important acts of worship. It is not used as a dead language here, a tongue "not understood of the people," but as a living force in the invisible worlds. It is not used to hide knowledge from the people, but in order that certain vibrations may be set up in the invisible worlds which cannot be set up in the ordinary languages of Europe, unless a great Occultist should compose in them the necessary successions of sounds. To translate a mantra is to change it from a "Word of Power" into an ordinary sentence; the sounds being changed, other sound-forms are created.

Some of the arrangements of Latin words, with the music wedded to them in Christian worship, cause the most marked effects in the supra-physical worlds, and anyone who is at all sensitive will be conscious of peculiar effects caused by the chanting of some of the most sacred sentences, especially in the Mass. Vibratory effects may be felt by anyone who will sit quiet and receptive as some of these sentences are uttered by priest or choristers. And at the same time effects are caused in the higher worlds directly affecting the subtle bodies of the worshippers in the way above described, and also appealing to the Intelligences in those worlds with a meaning as definite as the words addressed by one person to another on the physical plane, whether as prayer or, in some cases, as command. The sounds, causing active flashing forms, rise through the worlds, affecting the consciousness of the Intelligences residing in them, and bringing some of them to render the definite services required by those who are taking part in the church office.

Such mantras form an essential part of every Sacrament.

The next essential part of the Sacrament, in its outward and visible form, are certain gestures. These are called Signs, or Seals, or Sigils—the three words meaning the same thing in a Sacrament. Each sign has its own particular meaning, and marks the direction imposed on the invisible forces with which the celebrant is dealing, whether those forces be his own or poured through him. In any case, they are needed to bring about the desired result, and they are an essential portion of the sacramental rite. Such a sign is called a "Sign of Power," as the mantra is a "Word of Power."

It is interesting to read in occult works of the past references to these facts, true then as now, true now as then. In the Egyptian *Book of the Dead* is described the *post-mortem* journey of the Soul, and we read how he is stopped and challenged at various stages of that journey. He is stopped and challenged by the Guardians of the Gate of each successive world, and the Soul cannot pass through the Gate and go on his way unless he knows two things: he must pronounce a word, the Word of Power: he must make a sign, the Sign of Power. When that Word is spoken, when that Sign is given, the bars of the Gate fall down, and the Guardians stand aside to let the Soul pass through. A similar account is given in the great mystic Christian Gospel, the *Pistis Sophia*, before mentioned. Here the passage through the worlds is not of a Soul set free from the body by death, but of one who has voluntarily left it in the course of Initiation. There are great Powers, the Powers of Nature, that bar his way, and till the Initiate gives the Word and the Sign, they will not allow him to pass through the portals of their realms. This double knowledge, then, was necessary—to speak the Word of Power, to make the Sign of Power. Without these progress was blocked, and without these a Sacrament is no Sacrament.

Further, in all Sacraments some physical material is used, or should be used. This is ever a symbol of that which is to be gained by the Sacrament, and points to the nature of the "inward and spiritual grace" received through it. This is also the material means of conveying the grace, not symbolically, but actually, and a subtle change in this material adapts it for high ends.

Now a physical object consists of the solid, liquid, and gaseous particles into which a chemist would resolve it by analysis, and further of ether, which interpenetrates the grosser stuffs. In this ether play the magnetic energies. It is further connected with counterparts of subtle matter, in which play energies subtler than the magnetic, but like them in nature and more powerful.

When such an object is magnetised a change is effected in the ethereal portion, the wave-motions are altered and systematised, and made to follow the wave-motions of the ether of the magnetiser; it thus comes to share his nature, and the denser particles of the object, played on by the ether, slowly change their rates of vibration. If the magnetiser has the power of affecting the subtler counterparts also he makes them similarly vibrate in assonance with his own.

This is the secret of magnetic cures: the irregular vibrations of the diseased person are so worked on as to accord with the regular vibrations of the healthy operator, as definitely as an irregularly swinging object may be made to swing regularly by repeated and timed blows. A doctor will magnetise water and cure his patient therewith.

He will magnetise a cloth, and the cloth, laid on the seat of pain, will heal. He will use a powerful magnet, or a current from a galvanic cell, and restore energy to a nerve. In all cases the ether is thrown into motion, and by this the denser physical particles are affected.

A similar result accrues when the materials used in a Sacrament are acted on by the Word of Power and the Sign of Power. Magnetic changes are caused in the ether of the physical substance, and the subtle counterparts are affected according to the knowledge, purity, and devotion of the celebrant who magnetises—or, in the religious term, consecrates—it. Further, the Word and the Sign of Power summon to the celebration the Angels specially concerned with the materials used and the nature of the act performed, and they lend their powerful aid, pouring their own magnetic energies into the subtle counterparts, and even into the physical ether, thus reinforcing the energies of the celebrant. No one who knows anything of the powers of magnetism can doubt the possibility of the changes in material objects thus indicated. And if a man of science, who may have no faith in the unseen, has the power to so impregnate water with his own vital energy that it cures a physical disease, why should power of a loftier, though *similar*, nature be denied to those of saintly life, of noble character, of knowledge of the invisible? Those who are able to sense the higher forms of magnetism know very well that consecrated objects vary much in their power, and that the magnetic difference is due to the varying knowledge, purity, and spirituality of the priest who consecrates them. Some deny all vital magnetism, and would reject alike the holy water of religion and the magnetised water of medical science. They are consistent, but ignorant. But those who admit the utility of the one, and laugh at the other, show themselves to be not wise but prejudiced, not learned but one-sided, and prove that their want of belief in religion biases their intelligence, predisposing them to reject from the hand of religion that which they accept from the hand of science.

We thus see that the outer part of the Sacrament is of very great importance. Real changes are made in the materials used. They are made the vehicles of energies higher than those which naturally belong to them; persons approaching them, touching them, will have their own etheric and subtle bodies affected by their potent magnetism, and will be brought into a condition very receptive of higher influences, being tuned into accord with the lofty Beings connected with the Word and the Sign used in consecration; Beings belonging to the invisible world will be present during the sacramental rite, pouring out their benign and gracious influences; and thus all who are worthy participants in the ceremony—sufficiently pure and devoted to be tuned by the vibrations caused—will find their emotions purified and stimulated, their spirituality quickened, and their hearts filled with peace, by coming into such close touch with the unseen realities.

We have now to apply these general principles to concrete examples, and to see how they explain and justify the sacramental rites found in all religions.

It will be sufficient if we take as examples three out of the Seven Sacraments used in the Church Catholic. Two are recognised as obligatory by all Christians, although extreme Protestants deprive them of their sacramental character, giving them a declaratory and remembrance value only instead of a sacramental; yet even among them the heart of true devotion wins something of the sacramental blessing the head denies. The third is not recognised as even nominally a Sacrament by Protestant Churches, though it shows the essential signs of a Sacrament, as given in the definition in the Catechism of the Church of England already quoted. The first is that of Baptism; the second that of the Eucharist; the third that of Marriage. The putting of Marriage out of the rank of a Sacrament has much degraded its lofty ideal, and has led to much of that loosening of its tie that thinking men deplore.

The Sacrament of Baptism is found in all religions, not only at the entrance into earth-life, but more generally as a ceremony of purification. The ceremony which admits the new-born—or adult—incomer into a religion has a sprinkling with water as an essential part of the rite, and this was as universal in ancient days as it is now. The Rev. Dr. Giles remarks: "The idea of using water as emblematic of spiritual washing is too obvious to allow surprise at the antiquity of this rite. Dr. Hyde, in his treatise on the *Religion of the Ancient Persians*, xxxiv. 406, tells us that it prevailed among that people. 'They do not use circumcision for their children, but only baptism, or washing for the purification of the soul. They bring the child to the priest into the church, and place him in front of the sun and fire, which ceremony being completed, they look upon him as more sacred than before. Lord says that they bring the water for this purpose in bark of the Holm-tree; that tree is in truth the Haum of the Magi, of which we spoke before on another occasion. Sometimes also it is otherwise done by immersing him in a large vessel of water, as Tavernier tells us. After such washing, or baptism, the priest imposes on the child the name given by the parents." A few weeks after the birth of a Hindu child a ceremony is performed, a part of which consists in sprinkling the child with water—such sprinkling entering into all Hindu worship. Williamson gives authorities for the practise of Baptism in Egypt, Persia, Thibet, Mongolia, Mexico, Peru, Greece, Rome, Scandinavia, and among the Druids. Some of the prayers quoted are very fine: "I pray that this celestial water, blue and light blue, may enter into thy body and there live. I pray that it may destroy in thee, and put away from thee, all the things evil and adverse that were given to thee before the beginning of the world." "O child! receive the water of the Lord of the world who is our life: it is to wash and to purify; may these drops remove the sin which was given to thee before the creation of the world, since all of us are under its power."

Tertullian mentions the very general use of Baptism among non-Christian nations in a passage already quoted, and others of the Fathers refer to it.

In most religious communities a minor form of Baptism accompanies all religious ceremonies, water being used as a symbol of purification, and the idea being that no man should enter upon worship until he has purified his heart and conscience, the outer washing symbolising the inner lustration. In the Greek and Roman Churches a small receptacle for holy water is placed near every door, and every incoming worshipper touches it, making with it on himself the sign of the cross ere he goes onward towards the altar. On this Robert Taylor remarks: "The baptismal fonts in our Protestant churches, and we need hardly say more especially the little cisterns at the entrance of our Catholic chapels, are not imitations, but an unbroken and never interrupted continuation of the same *aqua minaria*, or *amula*, which the learned Montfaucon, in his *Antiquities*, shows to have been vases of holy water, which were placed by the heathens at the entrance of their temples, to sprinkle themselves with upon entering those sacred edifices."

Whether in the Baptism of initial reception into the Church, or in these minor lustrations, water is the material agent employed, the great cleansing fluid in Nature, and therefore the best symbol for purification. Over this water a mantra is pronounced, in the English ritual represented by the prayer, "Sanctify this water to the mystical washing away of sin," concluding with the formula, "In the name of the Father, and of the Son, and of the Holy Ghost. Amen." This is the Word of Power, and it is accompanied by the Sign of Power, the Sign of the Cross made over the surface of the water.

The Word and the Sign give to the water, as before explained, a property it previously had not, and it is rightly named "holy water." The dark powers will not approach it; sprinkled on the body it gives a sense of peace, and conveys new spiritual life. When a child is baptised, the spiritual energy given to the water by the Word and the Sign reinforces the spiritual life in the child, and then the Word of Power is again spoken, this time over the child, and the Sign is traced on his forehead, and in his subtle bodies the vibrations are felt, and the summons to guard the life thus sanctified goes forth through the invisible world; for this Sign is at once purifying and protective—purifying by the life that is poured forth through it, protective by the vibrations it sets up in the subtle bodies. Those vibrations form a guardian wall against the attacks of hostile influences in the invisible worlds, and every time that holy water is touched, the Word pronounced, and the Sign made, the energy is renewed, the vibrations are reinforced, both being recognised as potent in the invisible worlds, and bringing aid to the operator.

In the early Church, Baptism was preceded by a very careful preparation, those admitted to the Church being mostly converts from surrounding faiths. A convert passed through three definite stages of instruction, remaining in each grade till he had mastered its teachings, and he was then admitted to the Church by Baptism. Only after that was he taught the Creed, which was not committed to writing, nor ever repeated in the presence of an unbeliever; it thus served as a sign of recognition, and a proof of the position of the man who was able to recite it, showing that he was a baptised member of the Church. How truly in those days the grace conveyed by Baptism was believed in is shown by the custom of death-bed Baptism that grew up. Believing in the reality of Baptism, men and women of the world, unwilling to resign its pleasures or to keep their lives pure from stain, would put off the rite of Baptism until Death's hand was upon them, so that they might benefit by the sacramental grace, and pass through Death's portal pure and clean, full of spiritual energy. Against that abuse some of the great Fathers of the Church struggled, and struggled effectively. There is a quaint story told by one of them, I think by S. Athanasius, who was a man of caustic wit, not averse to the use of humour in the attempt to make his hearers understand at times the folly or perversity of their behaviour. He told his congregation that he had had a vision, and had gone up to the gateway of heaven, where S. Peter stood as Warder. No pleased smile had he for the visitant, but a frown of stern displeasure. "Athanasius," said he, "why are you continually sending me these empty bags, carefully sealed up, with nothing inside?" It was one of the piercing sayings we meet with in Christian antiquity, when these things were real to Christian men, and not mere forms, as they too often are to-day.

The custom of Infant Baptism gradually grew up in the Church, and hence the instruction which in the early days preceded Baptism came to be the preparation for Confirmation, when the awakened mind and intelligence take up and re-affirm the baptismal promises. The reception of the infant into the Church is seen to be rightly done, when man's life is recognised as being lived in the three worlds, and when the Spirit and Soul who have come to inhabit the new-born body are known to be not unconscious and unintelligent, but conscious, intelligent, and potent in the invisible worlds. It is right and just that the "Hidden Man of the heart" should be welcomed to the new stage of his pilgrimage, and that the most helpful influences should be brought to bear upon the vehicle in which he is to dwell, and which he has to mould to his service. If the eyes of men were opened, as were of old those of the servant of Elisha, they would still see the horses and chariots of fire gathered round the mountain where is the prophet of the Lord.

We come to the second of the Sacraments selected for study, that of the Sacrifice of the Eucharist, a symbol of the eternal Sacrifice already explained, the daily sacrifice of the Church Catholic throughout the world imaging that eternal Sacrifice by which the worlds were made, and by which they are evermore sustained. It is to be daily offered, as its archetype is perpetually existent, and men in that act take part in the working of the Law of Sacrifice, identify themselves with it, recognise its binding nature, and voluntarily associate themselves with it in its working in the worlds; in such identification, to partake of the material part of the Sacrament is necessary, if the identification is to be complete, but many of the benefits may be shared, and the influence going forth to the worlds may be increased, by devout worshippers, who associate themselves mentally, but not physically, with the act.

This great function of Christian worship loses its force and meaning when it is regarded as nothing more than a mere commemoration of a past sacrifice, as a pictorial allegory without a deep ensouling truth, as a breaking of bread and a pouring out of wine without a sharing in the eternal Sacrifice. So to see it is to make it a mere shell, a dead picture instead of a living reality. "The cup of blessing which we bless, is it not the communion [the communication of, the sharing in] of the blood of Christ?" asks the apostle. "The bread which we break, is it not the communion of the body of Christ?" And he goes on to point out that all who eat of a sacrifice become partakers of a common nature, and are joined into a single body, which is united to, shares the nature of, that Being who is, present in the sacrifice. A fact of the invisible world is here concerned, and he speaks with the authority of knowledge. Invisible Beings pour of their essence into the materials used in any sacramental rite, and those who partake of those materials—which become assimilated in the body and enter into its ingredients—are thereby united to those whose essence is in it, and they all share a common nature. This is true when we take even ordinary food from the hand of another—part of his nature, his vital magnetism, mingles with our own; how much more true then when the food has been solemnly and purposely impregnated with higher magnetisms, which affect the subtle bodies as well as the physical. If we would understand the meaning and use of the Eucharist we must realise these facts of the invisible worlds, and we must see in it a link between the earthly and the heavenly, as well as an act of the universal worship, a co-operation, an association, with the Law of Sacrifice, else it loses the greater part of its significance.

The employment of bread and wine as the materials for this Sacrament—like the use of water in the Sacrament of Baptism—is of very ancient and general usage. The Persians offered bread and wine to Mithra, and similar offerings were made in Tibet and Tartary. Jeremiah speaks of the cakes and the drink offered to the Queen of Heaven by the Jews in Egypt, they taking part in the Egyptian worship. In Genesis we read that Melchisedek, the King-Initiate, used bread and wine in the blessing of Abraham. In the various Greek Mysteries bread and wine were used, and Williamson mentions their use also among the Mexicans, Peruvians, and Druids.

The bread stands as the general symbol for the food that builds up the body, and the wine as symbol of the blood, regarded as the life-fluid, "for the life of the flesh is in the blood." Hence members of a family are said to share the same blood, and to be of the blood of a person is to be of his kin. Hence, also, the old ceremonies of the "blood-covenant"; when a stranger was made one of a family or of a tribe, some drops of blood from a member were transfused into his veins, or he drank them—usually mingled with water—and was thenceforth considered as being a born member of the family or tribe, as being of its blood. Similarly, in the Eucharist, the worshippers partake of the bread, symbolising the body, the nature, of the Christ, and of the wine symbolising the blood, the life of the Christ, and become of His kin, one with Him.

The Word of Power is the formula "This is My Body," "This is My Blood." This it is which works the change which we shall consider in a moment, and transforms the materials into vehicles of spiritual energies. The Sign of Power is the hand extended over the bread and the wine, and the Sign of the Cross should be made upon them, though this is not always done among Protestants. These are the outer essentials of the Sacrament of the Eucharist.

It is important to understand the change which takes place in this Sacrament, for it is more than the magnetisation previously explained, though this also is wrought. We have here a special instance of a general law.

By the occultist, a visible thing is regarded as the last, the physical, expression of an invisible truth. Everything is the physical expression of a thought. An object is but an idea externalised and densified. All the objects in the world are Divine ideas expressed in physical matter. That being so, the reality of the object does not lie in the outer form but in the inner life, in the idea that has shaped and moulded the matter into an expression of itself. In the higher worlds, the matter being very subtle and plastic, shapes itself very swiftly to the idea, and changes form as the thought changes. As matter becomes denser, heavier, it changes form less readily, more slowly, until, in the physical world, the changes are at their slowest in consequence of the resistance of the dense matter of which the physical world is composed. Let sufficient time be given, however, and even this heavy matter changes under the pressure of the ensouling idea, as may be seen by the graving on the face of the expressions of habitual thoughts and emotions.

This is the truth which underlies what is called the doctrine of Transubstantiation, so extraordinarily misunderstood by the ordinary Protestant. But such is the fate of occult truths when they are presented to the ignorant. The "substance" that is changed is the idea which makes a thing to be what it is; "bread" is not mere flour and water; the idea which governs the mixing, the manipulation, of the flour and water, that is the "substance" which makes it "bread," and the flour and the water are what are technically called the "accidents," the arrangements of matter that give form to the idea. With a different idea, or substance, flour and water would take a different form, as indeed they do when assimilated by the body. So also chemists have discovered that the same kind and the same number of chemical atoms may be arranged in different ways and thus become entirely different things in their properties, though the materials are unchanged; such "isomeric compounds" are among the most interesting of modern chemical discoveries; the arrangement of similar atoms under different ideas gives different bodies.

What, then, is this change of substance in the materials used in the Eucharist? The idea that makes the object has been changed; in their normal condition bread and wine are food-stuffs, expressive of the divine ideas of nutritive objects, objects fitted for the building up of bodies. The new idea is that of the Christ nature and life, fitted for the building up of the spiritual nature and life of man. That is the change of substance; the object remains unchanged in its "accidents," its physical material, but the subtle matter connected with it has changed under the pressure of the changed idea, and new properties are imparted by this change. They affect the subtle bodies of the participants, and attune them to the nature and life of the Christ. On the "worthiness" of the participant depends the extent to which he can be thus attuned.

The unworthy participant, subjected to the same process, is injuriously affected by it, for his nature, resisting the pressure, is bruised and rent by the forces to which it is unable to respond, as an object may be broken into pieces by vibrations which it is unable to reproduce.

The worthy partaker, then, becomes one with the Sacrifice, with the Christ, and so becomes at one with also, united to, the divine Life, which is the Father of the Christ. Inasmuch as the act of Sacrifice on the side of form is the yielding up of the life it separates from others to be part of the common Life, the offering of the separated channel to be a channel of the one Life, so by that surrender the sacrificer becomes one with God. It is the giving itself of the lower to be a part of the higher, the yielding of the body as an instrument of the separated will to be an instrument of the divine Will, the presenting of men's "bodies as a living sacrifice, holy, acceptable unto God." Thus it has been truly taught in the Church that those who rightly take part in the Eucharist enjoy a partaking of the Christ-life poured out for men. The transmuting of the lower into the higher is the object of this, as of all, Sacraments. The changing of the lower force by its union with the loftier is what is sought by those who participate in it; and those who know the inner truth, and realise the fact of the higher life, may in any religion, by means of its sacraments, come into fuller, completer touch with the divine Life that upholds the worlds, if they bring to the rite the receptive nature, the act of faith, the opened heart, which are necessary for the possibilities of the Sacrament to be realised.

The Sacrament of Marriage shows out the marks of a Sacrament as clearly and as definitely as do Baptism and the Eucharist. Both the outer sign and the inward grace are there. The material is the Ring—the circle which is the symbol of the everlasting. The Word of Power is the ancient formula, "In the Name of the Father, and of the Son, and of the Holy Ghost." The Sign of Power is the joining of hands, symbolising the joining of the lives. These make up the outer essentials of the Sacrament.

The inner grace is the union of mind with mind, of heart with heart, which makes possible the realisation of the unity of spirit, without which Marriage is no Marriage, but a mere temporary conjunction of bodies. The giving and receiving of the ring, the pronouncing of the formula, the joining of hands, these form the pictorial allegory; if the inner grace be not received, if the participants do not open themselves to it by their wish for the union of their whole natures, the Sacrament for them loses its beneficent properties, and becomes a mere form.

But Marriage has a yet deeper meaning; religions with one voice have proclaimed it to be the image on earth of the union between the earthly and the heavenly, the union between God and man. And even then its significance is not exhausted, for it is the image of the relation between Spirit and Matter, between the Trinity and the Universe. So deep, so far-reaching, is the meaning of the joining of man and woman in Marriage.

Herein the man stands as representing the Spirit, the Trinity of Life, and the woman as representing the Matter, the Trinity of formative material. One gives life, the other receives and nourishes it. They are complementary to each other, two inseparable halves of one whole, neither existing apart from the other. As Spirit implies Matter and Matter Spirit, so husband implies wife and wife husband. As the abstract Existence manifests in two aspects, as a duality of Spirit and Matter, neither independent of the other, but each coming into manifestation with the other, so is humanity manifested in two aspects—husband and wife, neither able to exist apart, and appearing together. They are not twain but one, a dual-faced unity. God and the Universe are imaged in Marriage; thus closely linked are husband and wife.

It is said above that Marriage is also an image of the union between God and man, between the universal and the individualised Spirits. This symbolism is used in all the great scriptures of the world—Hindu, Hebrew, Christian. And it has been extended by taking the individualised Spirit as a Nation or a Church, a collection of such Spirits knit into a unity. So Isaiah declared to Israel: "Thy Maker is thine Husband; the Lord of hosts is His name.... As the bridegroom rejoiceth over the bride, so shall thy God rejoice over thee." So S. Paul wrote that the mystery of Marriage represented Christ and the Church.

If we think of Spirit and Matter as latent, unmanifested, then we see no production; manifested together, there is evolution. And so when the halves of humanity are not manifested as husband and wife, there is no production of fresh life. Moreover, they should be united in order that there may be a growth of life in each, a swifter evolution, a more rapid progress, by the half that each can give to each, each supplying what the other lacks. The twain should be blended into one, setting forth the spiritual possibilities of man. And they show forth also the perfect Man, in whose nature Spirit and Matter are both completely developed and perfectly balanced, the divine Man who unites in his own person husband and wife, the male and female elements in nature, as "God and Man are one Christ."

Those who thus study the Sacrament of Marriage will understand why religions have ever regarded Marriage as indissoluble, and have thought it better that a few ill-matched pairs should suffer for a few years than that the ideal of true Marriage should be permanently lowered for all. A nation must choose whether it will adopt as its national ideal a spiritual or an earthly bond in Marriage, the seeking in it of a spiritual unity, or the regarding it as merely a physical union. The one is the religious idea of Marriage as a Sacrament; the other the materialistic idea of it as an ordinary terminable contract. The student of the Lesser Mysteries must ever see in it a sacramental rite.

Other Books in this Series and Related Titles

The Hebrew Talisman by Richard Harte (978–1–63118–607–3)

Early Masonic Symbolism by Manly P Hall (978–1–63118–606–6)

Nature Spirits and Elementals by Louise Off (978-1-63118-605-9)

Swedenborg Bifrons by H P Blavatsky (978-1-63118-604-2)

Practical Use of Psychic Powers by C W Leadbeater (978-1-63118-603-5)

Using White & Black Magic by C W Leadbeater (978-1-63118-602-8)

Jesus, the Last Great Initiate by Edouard Schure (978-1-63118-599-1)

Mysterious Wonders of Antiquity by Manly P Hall (978-1-63118-598-4)

Ancient Mysteries and Secret Societies by Manly P Hall (978–1–63118–597–7)

The Zodiac and Its Signs by Manly P Hall (978–1–63118–596–0)

Life and Teachings of Hermes Trismegistus by Manly P Hall (978–1–63118–595–3)

The Secrets of Doctor Taverner by Dion Fortune (978–1–63118–594–6)

Vegetarianism, Theosophy & Occultism by Leadbeater &c (978–1–63118–593–9)

Applied Theosophy by Henry S Olcott (978–1–63118–592–2)

Higher Consciousness by C W Leadbeater (978–1–63118–591–5)

Theories About Reincarnation and Spirits by H P Blavatsky (978–1–63118–590–8)

The Use and Power of Thought by C W Leadbeater (978–1–63118–589–2)

Commentary on the Pymander by G R S Mead (978–1–63118–588–5)

Hypnotism and Mesmerism by Annie Besant (978–1–63118–587–8)

Spirits of Various Kinds by Helena P Blavatsky (978–1–63118–586–1)

The Hidden Language of Symbolism by Annie Besant (978–1–63118–585–4)

Eastern Magic & Western Spiritualism by Henry S Olcott (978–1–63118–584–7)

Spiritual Progress and Practical Occultism by H P Blavatsky (978–1–63118–583–0)

Memory and Consciousness by Besant & Blavatsky (978–1–63118–582–3)

The Origin of Evil by Helena P Blavatsky (978–1–63118–581–6)

The Camp of Philosophy: Studies in Alchemy by Bloomfield (978–1–63118–580–9)

The Testaments of the Twelve Patriarchs (978–1–63118–579–3)

Occult or Exact Science? by Helena P Blavatsky (978–1–63118–578–6)

Occultism, Semi-Occultism & Pseudo Occultism by A Besant (978–1–63118–577–9)

The Fourth-Gospel and Synoptical Problem by G R S Mead (978–1–63118–576–2)

On the Bhagavad-Gita by T Subba Row &c (978–1–63118–575–5)

What Theosophy Does for Us by C W Leadbeater (978–1–63118–574–8)

Spiritual Life for Man by Annie Besant (978–1–63118–573–1)

The Mysteries by Annie Besant (978–1–63118–572–4)

Fundamental Ideas of Theosophy by Bhagwan Das (978–1–63118–571–7)

Dreams: What They Are and How They Are Caused (978–1–63118–570–0)

Communication Between Different Worlds by Annie Besant (978–1–63118–569–4)

Animism, Magic and the Omnipotence of Thought by S Freud (978–1–63118–568–7)

Buddhism by F Otto Schrader (978–1–63118–567–0)

Death by W W Westcott (978–1–63118–566–3)

The Religion of Theosophy by Bhagwan Das (978–1–63118–565–6)

The Spirit of Zoroastrianism by Henry S Olcott (978–1–63118–564–9)

The Brotherhood of Religions by Annie Besant (978–1–63118–563–2)

Fourth Book of Maccabees by Josephus (978-1-63118-562-5)

The Story of Ahikar by Ahiqar (978-1-63118-561-8)

Vision of the Spirit by C. Jinarajadasa (978-1-63118-560-1)

Occult Arts by William Q. Judge (978-1-63118-559-5)

Kali the Mother by Sister Nivedita (978-1-63118-558-8)

Love and Death by Sri Aurobindo (978–1–63118–557–1)

Times and Seasons Volume 1, Numbers 4-6 (978-1-63118-556-4)

Times and Seasons Volume 1, Numbers 1-3 (978-1-63118-555-7)

The Book of John Whitmer by John Whitmer (978-1-63118-554-0)

Interesting Account of Several Remarkable Visions (978-1-63118-553-3)

The Evening and Morning Star Volume 1, Numbers 11 & 12 (978-1-63118-552-6)

The Evening and Morning Star Volume 1, Numbers 1 & 2 (978-1-63118-547-2)

Private Diary of Joseph Smith 1832-1834 (978-1-63118-546-5)

An Address to All Believers in Christ Elder David Whitmer (978-1-63118-545-8)

A Manuscript on Far West by Reed Peck (978-1-63118-544-1)

The Story of Mormonism by James E Talmage (978-1-63118-543-4)

The Philosophy of Mormonism by James E Talmage (978-1-63118-542-7)

The Angel of the Prairies or A Dream of the Future (978-1-63118-541-0)

The Book of Abraham: Mormon History by George Reynolds (978-1-63118-540-3)

Pearl of Great Price by Joseph Smith (978-1-63118-539-7)

Taittiriya Upanishad and Commentary by Charles Johnston (978-1-63118-538-0)

Initiation and the Great Mysteries by C H Vail (978-1-63118-537-3)

Yoga Sutras of Patanjali and Commentary by Charles Johnston (978-1-63118-536-6)

Essays on Ancient Magic by Helena P Blavatsky (978-1-63118-535-9)

The Hidden Mysteries of Christianity by Annie Besant (978-1-63118-534-2)

The Historic, Mythic and Mystic Christ by Annie Besant (978-1-63118-533-5)

The Use of Evil by Annie Besant (978-1-63118-532-8)

The Inmost Light and Other Tales by Arthur Machen (978-1-63118-531-1)

The Eleusinian Mysteries by Dudley Wright (978-1-63118-530-4)

The Wendigo and Other Haunting Tales Algernon Blackwood (978-1-63118-529-8)

The Great God Pan by Arthur Machen (978-1-63118-528-1)

The Apocalypse of Peter by Peter (978-1-63118-527-4)

The Vision of Saint Paul the Apostle by Paul (978-1-63118-526-7)

The Comte de St. Germain: the Secret of Kings Cooper-Oakley (978-1-63118-525-0)

The Golden Chain of Homer by Anton Josef Kirchweger (978-1-63118-524-3)

With the Adepts or an Adventure Among the Rosicrucians (978-1-63118-523-6)

The Treasure of Atlantis by J Allan Dunn (978-1-63118-522-9)

Early Translation of the Acts of the Apostles by Luke (978-1-63118-521-2)

Book of Vexations by Paracelsus (978-1-63118-520-5)

Hermetic Arcanum by Jean d'Espagnet (978-1-63118-519-9)

A Weird Tale and Other Supernatural Stories by W Q Judge (978-1-63118-518-2)

The Secret Book of the Philosopher's Stone by Artephius (978-1-63118-517-5)

Initiation of the Great Pyramid by Manly P Hall (978-1-63118-516-8)

The A. E. Waite Reader: A Selection of Occult Essays (978-1-63118-515-1)

Freher's Process in the Philosophical Work by D A Freher (978-1-63118-514-4)

The Alchemical Catechism of Paracelsus by Paracelsus (978-1-63118-513-7)

The Life of Pythagoras by Porphyry (978-1-63118-512-0)

On the Philadelphian Gold by Philochrysus & Philadelphus (978-1-63118-511-3)

A Collection of Fiction and Essays by Occult Writers on Supernatural and Metaphysical Subjects by various (978-1-63118-510-6)

The Stone of the Philosophers by A E Waite (978-1-63118-509-0)

Freemasonry & Catholicism by Max Heindel (978-1-63118-508-3)

Aurora of the Philosophers by Paracelsus (978-1-63118-507-6)

Brothers and Builders by Joseph Fort Newton (978-1-63118-506-9)

On the Cave of the Nymphs in the Odyssey by Porphyry (978-1-63118-505-2)

The Symbols and Legends of Masonry by C H Vail (978-1-63118-504-5)

The Odes of Solomon by King Solomon (978-1-63118-503-8)

The Book of Wisdom of Solomon by King Solomon (978-1-63118-502-1)

The Sword of Welleran and Other Stories by Lord Dunsany (978-1-63118-501-4)

The Magician's Heavenly Chaos by Thomas Vaughan (978-1-63118-500-7)

The Devil in Love by Jacques Cazotte (978-1-63118-499-4)

Atlantis, the Gods of Antiquity and the Myth of the Dying God (978-1-63118-498-7)

Mandukya Upanishad and Commentary by Charles Johnston (978-1-63118-497-0)

Mundaka Upanishad and Commentary by Charles Johnston (978-1-63118-496-3)

Tao Te Ching & Commentary by Lao Tzu & C Johnston (978-1-63118-495-6)

Prashna Upanishad and Commentary by Charles Johnston (978-1-63118-494-9)

Katha Upanishad and Commentary by Charles Johnston (978-1-63118-493-2)

The Hymn of Jesus by G. R. S. Mead (978-1-63118-492-5)

Kena Upanishad and Commentary by Charles Johnston (978-1-63118-491-8)

Isha Upanishad and Commentary by Charles Johnston (978-1-63118-490-1)

Rosicrucians and Speculative Masonry in the Seventeenth Century (978-1-63118-489-5)

Audio versions are also available on Audible, Amazon and Apple

www.ingramcontent.com/pod-product-compliance
Lightning Source LLC
LaVergne TN
LVHW041502070426
835507LV00009B/767